Copyright © 2014 Joe Sinclair
All rights reserved.

ISBN: 1497543843
ISBN 13: 9781497543843
Library of Congress Control Number: 2014906545

CreateSpace Independent Publishing Platform
North Charleston, South Carolina

Other books by Joe Sinclair:

Putting Life on the Finish Line
The Marathon Called Educational Leadership
Queenie and Little Joe

Dedication

This book is dedicated to the memory of Earl and Peggy Bolden. They were the loving owners of Lulu the Snow Goat from Snow Camp. Special recognition and appreciation is extended to Don Bolden and my wife, Claryce, for their contributions to this true story about a Nubian goat with special animal instincts.

Special thanks to Carla Leslie for her assistance in preparing this book for publication.

Foreword

DR. JOE SINCLAIR WAS ALREADY a legend when I met him; little did I know that he would have a remarkable impact on me as an educational leader. His wisdom comes from successfully leading multiple school districts, a dedication to lifelong learning and fitness, and selflessly shepherding fellow educators along in their own journeys. I am grateful for his leadership and the nuggets of advice he shares.

"Dr. Snow Joe"—as you will come to know him in this book—shares the story of Lulu, a weather-predicting goat. Readers young and old will enjoy this true story. We can all identify with the decisions that have to be made about whether to call off school or not when the forecast is calling for bad weather. As you read, you will meet a goat whose prediction skills exceed those of the meteorologists.

Whether enjoying this nonfiction text as a family, as an individual student, or as a class, be prepared to fall in love with Lulu the Snow Goat. This story will likely prompt discussion, and perhaps research, around animal instincts and behaviors that are helpful to humans.

Thanks, Dr. Snow Joe, for sharing this endearing account with us.

Jan King
North Carolina Principal of the Year (2010)

Lulu the Snow Goat

Once upon a time, there was a Nubian goat named Lulu. She lived on a farm with her owners, Earl and Peggy, in Snow Camp, a rural community in North Carolina.

Lulu was a very special goat. She did many unusual things. She would eagerly watch for her owners to come home. She would then run to them and nudge their pockets with her nose, looking for a treat to eat!

However, the most unusual talent she had was predicting when a snowstorm was headed her way. She had a special nose that sniffed the air, telling her when snow was about to fall from the sky.

Lulu's favorite place to sleep was on the porch of an old house that stood on the farm.

If Lulu smelled snow coming when she sniffed the air, she would scamper off to the barn and make her bed in a pile of sweet hay.

Lulu would trot to the barn several hours before the snow began falling. She would make her bed in the cozy barn until the snowfall ended.

As soon as Lulu ran to the barn, Earl, the farmer, would pick up the phone and call Dr. Snow Joe, telling him to close his schools! Lulu was in the barn!

Since Dr. Snow Joe was the superintendent of schools, he had to make sure that thousands of students would be safe and warm during the cold winter days.

Lulu would never, ever go to the barn unless it was going to snow. Everybody would wait and watch the sky. And, sure enough, the snow would start falling just a few hours after Lulu went in the barn. She was always right!

Earl, the farmer, took good care of Lulu. He loved his goat very much. She worked very hard to help boys and girls stay safe, always sniffing the sky for snow.

When Earl called Dr. Snow Joe and told him that Lulu wanted him to close schools and keep children safe inside, Dr. Snow Joe didn't listen.

Early one morning, Earl called Dr. Snow Joe and told him to close schools because Lulu had gone to the barn. But once again, Dr. Snow Joe decided not to listen. He let the children go to school anyway.

Sure enough, a few hours later, snow began to fall, and the roads became a slippery mess! Dr. Snow Joe scrambled to close his schools, but the roads were already very icy and slick! All the students and teachers had a hard time getting back to their houses during the snowstorm.

Lulu the Snow Goat had tried to warn Dr. Snow Joe to close his schools, but he wouldn't listen. Lulu was right, and Dr. Snow Joe was wrong!

A few days later, Lulu trotted to the barn. Once again, in just a few hours, snow began to fall.

Yet, Dr. Snow Joe decided not to listen to Lulu.

Poor Dr. Snow Joe! He was wrong again! Snow began falling, and angry parents began to call him. Dr. Snow Joe was feeling really bad.

Dr. Snow Joe had been listening to the weatherman on television, who said there would be no snow. He had decided Lulu was wrong. But it was the weatherman who was wrong. Lulu was right!

Dr. Snow Joe had learned his lesson. He decided to listen to Earl and Lulu the next time instead of the television weatherman.

Late one morning while children were in school, Earl called Dr. Snow Joe to tell him Lulu had trotted to the barn. Snow was on its way! Dr. Snow Joe turned on his television and heard the weatherman say there would be no snow. What was he to do?

Dr. Snow Joe decided he would take Lulu's advice instead of the weatherman's. He decided to close schools. Parents listened to Dr. Snow Joe and came to pick up their children.

Some parents, though, were surprised that the schools were closing. They had been listening to the weatherman who had said there was no snow in the air.

Some parents called Dr. Snow Joe and laughed at his decision to close the schools. They said he had made a **big** mistake.

The parents didn't know that Dr. Snow Joe had a secret four-legged helper who knew when it was time to close the schools!

Snow **did** begin to fall, and those who had believed the weatherman learned that he was **wrong**! Lulu was right!

Lulu became loved by everyone, especially all the boys and girls. Soon, many people all over the country found out about the special goat. Lulu the Snow Goat from Snow Camp appeared on television. People read about her in newspapers and books. Everybody was hearing about Lulu, the amazing weather-predicting goat!

Children dreamed of Lulu visiting them at school. Many parents took them to the farm to see the famous goat.

The weathermen began to listen to Lulu. She was always right about when it would snow! Soon everyone learned to pay attention to Lulu and her amazing talent to predict snow.

Songs were written about Lulu. People came from far and wide to see her. Everyone began to listen to Lulu!

Dr. Snow Joe really liked Lulu and her amazing way of sniffing the air. Lulu liked it when Dr. Snow Joe visited her.

There were nine different times that Earl, the farmer, called Dr. Snow Joe to tell him that Lulu had trotted to the barn and it was going to snow.

Each time, Lulu was right! She became so famous that even the television weathermen started listening to her. They would go to Lulu's barn to see if she was there.

Earl, his brother Don, and Dr. Snow Joe decided to sell hundreds of "Lulu the Snow Goat" T-shirts, caps, towels, and cups. All the money was given to students who needed help to go to college!

Not only did she keep the students safe, but Lulu also helped to send many boys and girls to college! Lulu was a hero!

The True Story of Lulu the Snow Goat
Reflections by Dr. Joe Sinclair

IN THE EARLY-MORNING HOURS OF a very cold winter day in 1987, I received a telephone call that would lead to national recognition and the beginning of a legend. My friend Earl Bolden, a farmer and good friend who lived on a farm in a rural area of southern Alamance County, found it necessary to rustle me out of a sound sleep with an early-morning telephone call to tell me that Lulu had gone to the barn. I struggled to get my eyes open and make sense of the conversation, and I asked Earl, "Who is Lulu, and what does a barn have to do with it?" And so the legend of Lulu was born.

Lulu the Snow Goat became famous when I learned to put my trust in the animal when deciding whether or not to close schools due to bad weather. Lulu, it seemed, never went to the barn unless it was going to snow, and she was amazingly right on the mark.

As I continued the conversation with Earl, I argued that even though it was cloudy and cold that morning, the weatherman had not predicted any snow for the day. Earl again cautioned me that Lulu never, ever went to the barn unless it was going to snow, and I could expect it in four to six hours. I listened for another minute or so, then politely ended the conversation. By this time, my wife, Claryce, was also awake and curious as to why someone would call in the wee hours of the morning. I told her that it was Earl, advising me to close schools because his goat went to the barn. We both laughed and went back to bed. Four hours later, at around eight o'clock, the snow started falling, ice covered the streets, and school buses were in ditches everywhere. Parents began calling and cursing, upset with the idiot superintendent who had not closed schools. A few minutes later, Earl called again, reminding me that I should have listened to him and closed schools.

Less than two weeks later, I received another early-morning phone call. Once again, Earl warned that Lulu had gone to the barn and that schools needed to be closed for the day. Still leery, I had seen the weather report from the night before, which predicted no snow, just cloudy, cold conditions. I politely listened, then again ignored the advice. Just as Lulu predicted, around seven thirty that morning—with all the buses on the roads and drivers busy picking up students—a snowfall began blanketing the city, causing terrible and unsafe travel conditions in a matter of minutes. I found myself having to scramble to close schools while taking another barrage of phone calls from irate parents. By this time, I had become very frustrated at trying to predict the weather for my role as school superintendent. Meanwhile, Lulu, the amazing animal that was perfect in her weather predictions, made the area weathermen—and me—appear as ill-informed goats.

The following week, the unusually cold winter produced yet another identical early-morning weather crisis. Earl made his usual phone call at four o'clock that morning, and although the weatherman did not have snow in the forecast, I took the time to look at radar predictions, which indicated possible precipitation about eighty miles south of Burlington. No schools were closing anywhere in central North Carolina, but I decided to take a chance and heed directions from Lulu the Snow Goat. I called radio and television stations to announce the school closings. At the office, everyone was in shock as to my decision when no snow was even falling and questioned me as to why I would do such a thing. I simply replied, "You don't understand, but I'll tell you later," and held my breath for hours in hopes Lulu was right. Sure enough, between seven and eight o'clock, ice and snow quickly paralyzed the entire area. Reporters and other superintendents were calling from all over central North Carolina wanting to know how I knew to call off school that day.

Don Bolden, Earl's brother and a personal friend, was also the editor of the *Burlington Times-News*, a daily newspaper that served central North Carolina. When I revealed that I was using Lulu as my weather forecaster for closing schools, Don began writing detailed stories about this very unusual, very accurate, furry weather-predictor. Immediately after, many of the stories became a local hit, Lulu was famous, and the Associated Press wire service soon picked up the stories to share nationwide. Over the next two years, Lulu went to the barn on nine different occasions, and each time, I closed schools because of the impending snow. Local television stations conducted their evening weather telecasts from Earl's farm and interviewed Earl, his wife, Peggy, and me. They were curious to know more about Lulu and her whereabouts around the barnyard during the broadcast.

One evening, the WXII television station, based in Winston-Salem, North Carolina, was conducting a live telecast from Earl's farm. Lulu was nowhere to be seen, but Earl had learned a little secret. If he offered Lulu a little taste of tobacco, she would immediately come out of hiding to investigate. Sure enough, as the program was airing live for thousands of viewers waiting for a sight of Lulu on that cold winter evening, the reporter noticed Earl reach into his pocket and pull out a cigarette. Immediately, Lulu trotted out to appear in front of the cameras, ready to feast on the tasty treat.

The startled reporter asked Earl, "Is that a carrot you are feeding Lulu?"

"No," replied Earl. "It's cigarettes."

"Cigarettes?" asked the shocked reporter. "What kind of cigarettes?"

With his dry sense of humor and his slow, Southern drawl, Earl replied, "Well, it's either Winston's or Salem's."

With that response, the entire television crew for the Winston-Salem news station enjoyed a good laugh as Lulu chewed away.

Lulu became so popular that I couldn't go into a restaurant in Burlington without conversations immediately turning to the goat and her remarkable instinct for predicting snow. On cold winter evenings, waitresses and patrons alike would want to know if Lulu had gone to the barn. Several school superintendents in nearby school districts would routinely call me on questionable weather mornings to inquire about Lulu's whereabouts. They would always ask me to keep their call a secret, just in case their board members would find out that they, too, were seeking a goat's advice about closing schools.

The news media absolutely went crazy over Lulu the Snow Goat. *Star Magazine* sent a reporter to Earl's farm to interview both Earl and me and published a picture of Lulu, Earl, and me for their publication. When the popular magazine began selling in the Burlington area, it was fun to tell my humorous friends which character was Lulu and which was me in the picture. In addition to numerous local news articles, newspapers across the country also picked up the story. I conducted many television and radio interviews for stations throughout the United States, one coming from a popular radio station reporter in Los Angeles, California, who wanted to know if Lulu was also able to predict earthquakes and dust storms. Reporters at a station in Birmingham, Alabama, asked if Lulu could help solve drought conditions by predicting rain. National Public Radio (NPR) also featured several segments about Lulu and her uncanny ability to predict the weather.

Lulu was mentioned on several national television shows, including *Good Morning America*. The American Broadcasting Company (ABC) was considering a story to be included on its Sunday evening nationwide program called *Incredible Sundays*. Congressman Howard Coble from Greensboro presented our school district with an American flag, which had flown over the capitol, in honor of Lulu the Snow Goat.

Songs about Lulu were written and sung on local radio stations, and ballads about Lulu were becoming popular in the Burlington area. Local teachers did an evaluation of Lulu's skills and deemed her "outstanding" in her field of expertise. Earl and Peggy received letters from goat owners in other states who compared their pet goats to Lulu. While all of this national attention was focused on Lulu's snow-predicting abilities, Don and Earl decided, with my input, to create a Lulu the Snow Goat Scholarship Fund for Needy Kids.

We decided to capitalize on the goat's popularity to raise money and send deserving high school seniors to college. Don, Earl, and Peggy came up with the idea of selling Lulu the Snow Goat shirts, cups, pins, coffee mugs, and many other usable articles. The Burlington City Board of Education, a group of very supportive people, even wore the Snow Goat shirts one night at a board meeting. Orders were placed to manufacturers, and the process of selling the Lulu shirts throughout the area began. Retail stores eagerly sponsored the sale of the special items, and volunteers held Saturday sales in various shopping centers. Thousands of dollars were raised through merchandise sales, which allowed four very deserving students to receive college scholarships. Each received his or her Lulu Scholarship in a special presentation by the educational sorority Alpha Delta Kappa–ETA Chapter.

Earl, the farmer and great friend, became very popular with schoolchildren in the area. He was very much in demand and went into classrooms and talked with students about Lulu and her animal instincts. The story became a true-life science lesson for many students. Many would visit Earl and Peggy's farm in hopes of catching a glimpse of Lulu.

Never has a Nubian goat contributed so much in her own way to so many people. Her instincts helped to keep students and staff safe, and her fame sent deserving students to college. Her entire legacy helped bring joy to the hearts of thousands throughout America in need of a feel-good success story to brighten their days.

The Study of Animal Instincts

EARL BOLDEN WAS A VERY smart man. I often had discussions with him about animal instincts and how to interpret an animal's behavior. Earl said that he had studied Lulu's habits for several years to determine what her actions meant for certain weather predictions. Earl said he didn't train Lulu; Lulu trained him—to know how to interpret her actions in certain situations. It is a fact that animals have a keen instinct that humans lack for sensing change or danger. At the time of Lulu's great popularity, Earl enjoyed taking this story into the elementary classrooms and talking with students about animal behavior and how they could learn from it.

Top Left: Earl receives an award from Dr. Snow Joe
Top Right: Peggy, Lulu, and Earl in front of TV cameras
Bottom: Dr. Snow Joe seeks advice from Lulu the Snow Goat

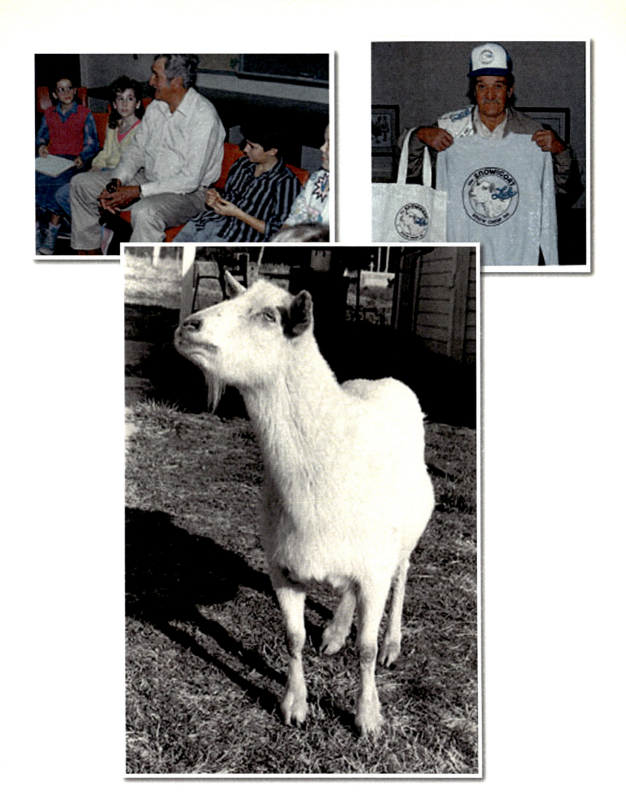

Top Left: Earl meets with children at school to teach them about animal instincts
Top Right: Earl holding items about Lulu the Snow Goat used for the scholarship fund
Bottom: Lulu sniffing the air for snow

About the Author

Joe Sinclair is an author, educator, and athlete. He has spent his entire life in an educational environment. His father and mother were career educators, and Joe has devoted more than forty-five years of his life to helping young people in the educational process.

The former North Carolina Superintendent of the Year is the author of *Putting Life on the Finish Line*, which details his outstanding career as a marathon runner and advisor. He is also the author of *The Marathon Called Educational Leadership*, which details his very successful and very unusual career in educational leadership (additional information about the true story of Lulu the Snow Goat is contained in this publication).

Joe holds a BS degree in health and physical education from Appalachian State University, MS degrees in physical education and school administration from North Carolina A & T State University, an EdS in educational leadership from Western Carolina University, and an EdD in educational leadership from the University of North Carolina at Greensboro.

He and his wife, Claryce, reside in Statesville, North Carolina.

Made in the USA
Middletown, DE
09 November 2014